# STRESSPOINTS:

## A Young Person's Guide to Peace of Heart

*by Douglas Fazzina and Joseph Moore*

Paulist Press
New York and Mahwah

Library of Congress Cataloging-in-Publication Data

Fazzina, Douglas, 1963-
Stresspoints : a young person's guide to peace of heart / by
Douglas Fazzina and Joseph Moore.
p.    cm.
Summary: Discusses, from a Christian point of view, fifteen causes
of stress, including self-esteem, depression, consumerism, and
divorce and offers suggestions on finding inner peace through
sharing feelings, diet and exercise, prayer, and meditation.
ISBN 0-8091-2983-3 (pbk.)
1. Youth—Conduct of life.   2. Stress (Psychology)—Juvenile
literature.   3. Youth—Religious life.   [1. Stress (Psychology)
2. Conduct of life.   3. Christian life.]   I. Moore, Joseph, 1944-
II. Title.   III. Title: Stress points.
BJ1661.F35   1988
248.8'3—dc19   88-5913 CIP AC

Published by Paulist Press
997 Macarthur Blvd.
Mahwah, N.J.  07430

Printed and bound in the
United States of America

# CONTENTS

# ACKNOWLEDGEMENTS

We would like to thank Nancy Spenser, John Krisiukenas, and Michael Adams for their contributions as young people to this work, and especially Mark Ferreira for both his poems and his encouragement.

For
Kerry and Ryan

# INTRODUCTION

"Down in the dumps," "Bummed out," "Ticked off" . . . we have a hundred metaphors in English for depicting inner feelings of anger, depression and rejection. But often these expressions are unclear and signify different things to different people. More important than *others* understanding us is that we understand ourselves. One of the major problems of emotional pain is that we don't understand what's going on inside of us . . . and this is where psychology is helpful. And so we will explore some insights from psychologists about what makes people tick. But psychology is able to only go so far. Sometimes even after we understand our feelings we still experience pain. And this is where our faith comes into play with its focus on Jesus the healer, the meaning of suffering and the role of the Christian community.

Teenage years are difficult emotionally. Your body is undergoing changes, emotions tend to be very intense, and a person is an inner jumble of feelings relating both to childhood and adulthood. All the more reason to try to "get a grip" at this stage in your life.

In the first part of the book, "STRESSPOINTS," we discuss fifteen points of stress which affect many teenagers. Even if there is one you don't relate to directly, it probably does touch the life of someone you know. In the second section, "STRESSBREAK-ERS," we make a half-a-dozen suggestions for finding more inner peace than you might presently be experiencing.

Part I

# STRESSPOINTS

# *Stresspoint #1:*

## SELF-ESTEEM

> *How still and sad the music of my heart sounds when I've been forgetting who I am. The song is slow and moving—almost painful. The song sings to me of the things that have been locked away inside of me. As the rhythm beats on I unlock these feelings. It feels so good when I get in touch with myself.*
>
> [*Nancy*]

A study was conducted of 28,000 high school seniors who were interviewed two years after graduation. Almost all of them reported that their self-esteem improved once they were out of high school! What does this say about our schools? Well, I think it says that there are very powerful ideas about being acceptable, popular and "cool" in high schools, and either you make it or you don't. There are defined ideas of groups, and people are judged by who their friends are. Certain behaviors are ridiculed in high school, and other behaviors are applauded. It is a very rigid place. And a kid's self-esteem plays into what is socially acceptable. And even though many of us would like to think we are above this, we really aren't. So of course after we graduate and this social world which has dominated our lives falls apart, we are amazed that out in the world people have other ideas of what's cool and what isn't. A kid who was made fun of might be very successful in the business world and win the respect of many. And, conversely, a kid who was a hero or a girl who was really popular might be seen in two years as someone just hanging around the old hometown not going anywhere in life. I'm not putting down staying in our hometown; I'm just trying to say that our ideas of successful human beings and failures change very quickly once we get away from the social milieu of high school. So bear this in mind if you feel you aren't with the "in group" at this point in time. The "in group" will soon be "out."

Today's culture is very concerned with the self. We hear a lot about self-image, self-fulfillment, "be good to yourself." Many older adults feel that younger people are getting more and more selfish and self-centered. And perhaps this is true. But all this preoccupation with the self isn't what we mean by self-esteem. A lot of this other stuff has to do with things outside ourselves; for example, if I have a good tan or I drive a hot sports car or I have nice clothes or I make a lot of money, then I feel good about myself, then I have worth. This is a shallow sense of the self because if I remove any of those *things* that give me a sense of security, then my self-image really crashes downward. Even being with the right friends should not be the source of our self-esteem. Self-esteem comes from within. It is an inner feeling that I am basically a good, worthwhile and lovable human being and I am worthy of the concern of others. Self-esteem isn't selfishness because when I feel good about myself I'm more able to reach out in love and friendship to other people. Psychologists say that self-esteem basically is given to us by our parents, but the teenage years can definitely add to or decrease self-worth. Here are a few suggestions for struggling to be yourself:

1. Try the best you can to be comfortable with who you are, beginning with how you look. There's nothing wrong with trying to improve on looks (such as by losing weight, wearing makeup or attractive clothing), but remember that improvement only goes to a point. At some point you need to accept yourself as you are, remembering that beauty is cultivated more in the

personality than in the body. A person may look great but have a lousy personality (you may know someone like this).

2. Grow to appreciate your interests and talents. Try not to become absorbed into what everybody else likes and does. Love your uniqueness and grow in it. Surround yourself with people who reinforce and encourage these special parts of you. Listen to the positive voices, not the negative ones.

3. Get feedback from other people about how you are coming across. A great way to do this might be to go on a teenage retreat where there is a lot of personal sharing and discussion. Ask other people for their feelings about and reactions to you: your looks, your talents and interests, your behavior, your interactions with other people. Getting good feedback from caring, trusted people is one of the best ways to continue to develop a positive self-esteem during the teenage years.

## DEPRESSION

*I feel like the sun when*
*it stops shining,*
*the moon when it goes in.*
*I feel like a song that*
*has no name, a lamp*
*that has no lightbulb,*
*a picture that has no meaning,*
*but most of all I feel pain.*

[*Mark*]

*I*t's so hard to know just what makes us tick on the inside, isn't it? We can talk about how we feel by descriptions like the one above, but we often don't understand why.

Commonly we call the experience which Mark is describing "depression" or feeling "down." It's when the excitement goes out of life and nothing seems very special and everything seems pretty boring. When people try to talk us out of this state of mind it usually doesn't work.

While the way we experience or feel depressed is unique to each of us, there are some common factors we can discuss. First of all, psychology offers us some insights. Much depression is caused, we are told, by unexpressed anger. In other words, when we feel really outraged by a teacher's attitude, for example, but we repress expressing that anger, later on we might feel depressed and not realize that it's connected to unexpressed anger felt earlier in the day. Now this might sound surprising to you because the two emotions feel very different. But psychologists are really on to something here. A kid who lives in a situation in which he or she is constantly angry (intense dislike for a stepparent, for example) is often depressed most of the time. When we talk about anger we'll reflect upon the need to express that anger in appropriate ways in order to avoid depression.

Psychologists today increasingly think that other kinds of depression, especially the deep, long-lasting kinds, can be the result of a chemical imbalance in a person. In other words, there can be biological reasons for creating depressed feelings or for making a psychological depression more intense. A young person who has long periods of depression (for a week or more) really should get checked out by a medical doctor. If depression is physical it can be pretty much brought back to a more manageable state by the temporary use of anti-depressant medication.

Another form of depression can be brought on by over-eating or eating all the wrong kinds of food. Sometimes kids who eat poorly also fail to exercise, which creates a fatigue, which adds to the depression. Then if we put on weight as a result of our diet and lack of exercise we might feel lousy about ourself, which adds to the down feelings. See how interconnected we are with everything we do and experience. We are one body-spirit or soul. What we do to our body affects our souls and vice versa. When we are "clean" living, health conscious in terms of diet and exercise, we find that our inner spirit is tremendously energized! There is an old adage that "we are what we eat." How true that is; we are who we are by *all* that we "take in," both physically and emotionally.

We also are what we drink. Ingesting chemicals like alcohol, cocaine and hallucinogens has an afterward component, a delayed reaction called depression. In the advanced stages of drug abuse (like alcoholism) people keep getting "high" to avoid the downward spiral of feelings when the drug wears off. A major word of caution here is that drugs like alcohol and cocaine should particularly not be used when we are feeling low already. Why?

Because the drug will only eventually *add* to our feelings of depression. The temporary relief offered is not worth the pain to follow.

How often we say that we are depressed but we don't know why. We aren't lying to ourselves . . . it's just that we can't make the connection between feelings and events by ourselves. And the only way we can make the connection very often is by talking about our feelings with someone else, with a friend. I know a kid named Ed who is very macho and likes to keep all his feelings inside. "I can solve my own problems within my own head . . . I think things out . . . " he told me. In my judgment this privatized approach to problem solving is not too effective. I notice that my friend Ed is still pretty depressed most of the time. What does that say? Sure, there are difficult situations and decisions in life which all of us have to at some time deal with on our own, but depression is not something that gets resolved in isolation. In fact the longer we stay isolated the longer the depression lasts.

Now people will try to "cheer us up" when we're down, saying, for example, "Come on, go out with us—you'll feel better." Occasionally this type of thing will be helpful temporarily to get our mind off our own problems. But the best thing we can say to someone who is depressed (or have said to us) is: "Come on, tell me about what's going on with you. What are you feeling?" Now we are often reluctant to respond because either we're so depressed we don't feel like talking, or we just don't think it will do any good, or we just can't figure out our feelings. But it is precisely by making ourselves talk to a good listener that we may unlock the key to deeper feelings.

I remember talking to a boy in my office one evening who had been depressed all day and didn't know why. So we retraced all the events of his day, only to discover that in homeroom that morning a girl he had thought was interested in him snubbed him when he said "hello." At the time he brushed it off, but deep down it really disappointed and hurt him and ate away at him until he got really depressed. But somehow he hadn't connected the depression with homeroom. Now, of course, realizing *why* he was depressed didn't take away the snub he received, but it did help. First of all, just talking about how hurt he felt was helpful to him. It also made him aware not only of disappointment in her but anger he felt at her rudeness and rejection, an anger he had repressed rather quickly. Secondly, just realizing *why* he felt so low was helpful. Understanding our negative feelings is the first step to getting rid of them.

## PARENTS

*Dear Mom and Dad . . .*

*Thinking back on my life, a vision of you appears. The three of us taking the time to love one another. It was so simple then. You carried me through the changing tides of my life, and now it must end. It's time for me to wade in the waters of my time, but all I want to do is bathe in your gentle lore. Goodbye, and thank you.*

*[Nancy]*

A great source of stress for many kids is parents. Part of the stress comes just from living so closely together. There will always be tensions between people in the same house. Another part of the stress is that parents have authority over you. And a third natural stress is that this authority over you is now occurring at a time in your life when you want to break away from other people making decisions about your life. And so, in summary, stress in this area is very normal.

But sometimes, in some households, there is more stress than need exist. It could be conflict with one or more parents or a single parent or a stepparent or guardian. Today's society has many styles of family life. At the root of most conflicts is a lack of communication. I know, this sounds pretty trite and you've heard that before, and so have I. But a relatively new study of 8,000 kids and their parents (Search Institute's "Young Adolescents and Their Parents," 1984) has convinced me once again that lack of communication is still the major problem. For example, this study found that the thing kids want *most* to talk to parents about is how they and their parents get along. But parents don't realize this. In fact it's not even on the list of things about which parents wish to talk to their kids! And why don't they know? Because their children don't tell them, of course. Listen, you're getting older now. You can't sit back and wait for your parents (or anyone) to bring up a topic you wish to discuss. No, *you* bring it up . . . it's your responsibility.

There's a lot going on in teenagers . . . true. That's what this little book is all about. But there's a lot going on in parents as well. Sometimes children don't realize this. Many parents who have trouble with teenagers not obeying rules interpret this rebellion as rejection. They are sometimes afraid that their children don't love them anymore. They don't fully understand that the rejection of rules isn't a rejection of them personally. They don't realize this because their children don't tell them! Similarly, sometimes because friends are so important to you at this age you are never home, never with the family, always out. Parents can be hurt by this absence and also feel rejected, no longer cherished. They don't understand because no one tells them.

Now I'm not putting all the burden on teenagers. Parents can be just as guilty as kids. When parents get hurt they often express anger. Some parents (especially fathers) are afraid to be open and vulnerable about their feelings with their children. They have probably been taught by their own parents' example that a parent shouldn't show weakness in front of children. With our understanding of psychology we wouldn't agree with this, but try to realize that your parents grew up in a different world. Maybe it's more difficult for them to open up than it is for you due to their upbringing.

My best suggestion is to try at your age to shift your relationship from being a kid to being more of a friend with your parent or parents. This is done by sharing life together. Not just sharing the same house but sharing lives. Ask them about themselves, their day, their dreams, their plans, their disappointments. Soak in from them the wisdom that living life has brought them. And talk about yourself: your day, school, your own hopes and fears. Show them signs of appreciation, like a "thank you" for a nicely cooked meal. Tell them on occasion how much they mean to you, how grateful you are for all they do. People of every age need a little gratitude now and then. Occasionally stay home with them or attend a family function, not because it's what you prefer but because you want to work at developing a long-lasting friendship with your folks. This becomes harder to do if you're a phantom all during your teenage years.

As far as rules, curfew and authority goes I would remind you that parents only make rules because they love their children and want to protect them from harm. Some parents are over-protective. I won't argue that. But when you have conflicts try to negotiate solutions where you give in a little to help arrive at solutions you both can live with. If your parents are still rigid and inflexible, try to love them anyway and forgive them and work at winning their trust by behaving maturely. Nothing breaks a parent's heart more than when trust is broken. The rebuilding of trust is a long, painful process. Think ahead of time and don't subject either your parents *or* yourself to that process.

## SUFFERING

*They go through my head confusing me.*
*My head spins round and round.*
*Where do they come from? . . .*
*Are they there to help me*
*Or are they there to hurt me?*
*I don't think I will ever know.*
*But they are my thoughts.*

[*Mark*]

Why? This automatic response to human suffering is the most common human response. It is difficult to understand how an all loving God can allow his creatures to undergo pain. That's a big philosophical question that I'll look at in a minute.

But first, let's look at suffering and stress. Many of us spend all our time running away from suffering. We act as though it isn't really a part of the "good life," and we pretend it can be avoided. Well the fact is, it can't be totally avoided. First of all, we have vulnerable human bodies which suffer disease and pain and eventually die and corrupt. We are not 100% together and whole psychologically, and so we suffer loneliness, poor self-esteem and depression. If we are truly forming relationships with other people, that human interaction and growth will also cause moments of pain as it does moments of joy. The sooner we accept that suffering is inevitably a part of human life, then the less stressful we will be. This doesn't mean we should desire to suffer or like to suffer, but it does mean that we will cease fleeing suffering. People who run from suffering sometimes do so by not thinking about painful problems or by not talking about them when they need to, others try to avoid pain by drugs or other strong distractions, while still others hold back from forming close relationships so as to avoid any future pain.

There are lots of things said about suffering—some helpful and some not. Suffering is not a problem to be solved. It's not a question to be answered. It's a mystery. A person cannot come up with a one-to-one solution to suffering, not a detailed answer that "explains" what is happening. Nonetheless, there are approaches which can help us to cope with this mystery. For one thing, our Christian faith can be a source of comfort. Jesus has promised to respond to our requests for help. There are many helpful texts in the New Testament. As an example, two are quoted here:

> My brothers, consider yourselves fortunate when all kinds of trials come your way, for you know that when your faith succeeds in facing such trials, the result is the ability to endure. Make sure that your endurance carries you all the way without failing, so that you may be perfect and complete, lacking nothing (Jas 1:2–4).

> Let us give thanks to the God and Father of our Lord Jesus Christ, the merciful Father, the God from whom all help comes! He helps us in all our troubles, so that we are able to help others who have all kinds of troubles, using the same help that we ourselves have received from God. Just as we have a share in Christ's many sufferings, so also through Christ we share in God's great help. If we suffer, it is for your help and salvation; if we are helped, then you too are helped and given the strength to endure with patience the same sufferings that we also endure. So our hope in you is never shaken;

we know that just as you share in our sufferings, you also share in the help we receive (2 Cor 1:3–7).

There is also much insight into human suffering which can be found in literature. Note the wisdom in this little poem by Robert Browning Hamilton:

> I walked a mile with Pleasure,
> She chattered all the way;
> But left me none the wiser
> For all she had to say.
>
> I walked a mile with Sorrow,
> And ne'er a word said she;
> But, oh, the things I learned from her
> When Sorrow walked with me!

Here are a few further reflections on suffering which you might find helpful.

1. Does God actually send certain sufferings to certain people? Does he plot our misery? Some people may think so because of early childhood experiences or because of remarks by parents and teachers. But such a concept does not square with what Jesus has revealed. The God whom Jesus revealed is Love itself. A loving father never sends deliberate misery. We suffer in both mind and body because of the vulnerability of the human condition (that is, because of original sin). We certainly do not suffer because God likes to see us in pain.

2. Do we suffer in this life for our sins? The answer to this question is both yes and no. We do not suffer for our sins in the way the ancient Jews thought. For example, when the ancient Jews were struck by famine, they would interpret the disaster as a punishment from God for misbehavior. This primitive

way of thinking was too simple; God does not act in that way. To put it in more concrete terms, God doesn't see to it that we stub our toe after we've said a swear word. We do suffer in this life for our sins, however, in the sense that sin and unkindness have their own way of bringing misery into our lives. The saying is true that we begin our heaven or hell here on earth.

3. Of what value is human suffering? This question can be approached from many angles. The value does not lie in the suffering itself but in the attitude with which we approach it. Two axioms apply here. The first axiom is: When we pray to be delivered from suffering, God often changes us rather than the situation. The second axiom is that outstanding piece of advice: " . . . to accept what I must, change what I can, and have the wisdom to know the difference."

Of course, the highest value of human suffering is that of serving the good of another human being. Jesus' own death for us is a witness to that.

# THE FUTURE

*You ask whether your verses are good. You ask me. You have asked others before. You send them to magazines. You compare them with other poems, and you are disturbed when certain editors reject your efforts. Now—I beg you to give up all that. You are looking outward and that above all you should not do now—go into yourself, search for the reason that bids you to write; find out whether it is spreading out its roots in the deepest places of your heart, acknowledge to yourself whether you would have to die if it were denied you to write. This above all—ask yourself in the stillest hour of your night: must I write?*

[*Rainer Maria Rilke,*
*"Letters to a Young Poet"*]

*B*efore beginning a discussion concerning the future, let's define what we mean when we use the term. The future could mean a year, a month, a day or even an hour from now. No matter how we use the word, thinking about what the future may hold for you can be very stressful. The context in which I'll discuss the future will concern what occurs after high school. The future may not be an issue for you at all, but if it is something you do think or worry about, I hope you'll find this section helpful.

The pressure you may be feeling at this point in your life may seem unbearable. It might seem that everyone is concerned about what you are going to do with the rest of your life. Are you going

19

to graduate, go to college, get a job, learn a trade or skill? If you are going to college, are your grades good enough, do you have the money, and, above all, where are you going to go? At some point in every teenager's life, these questions will undoubtedly arise. Usually these questions causing stress come from peers, guidance counselors and parents.

As teenagers in high school you are in a very unique situation. You may sometimes feel as though you are being treated like a kid, yet when the future is considered, you are forced to make very adult decisions. The future holds something very unique and special for everyone, including you. The first thing I would suggest is that you deal with and face the future head-on. It is not something that will magically disappear. Secondly, although it may not seem apparent, your parents, as well as your school counselors, are trying to help you get ready for and choose what is best for you.

I know you may have some fears or anxieties about the future. On the other hand your parents, friends or school counselors might be more uptight about your future than *you* are! In either case, it can help a great deal to talk to these people about what the future holds for you. If you haven't already, try to begin early to think about the next few years of your life. Guidance counselors are there to help students work out plans for the future. Try to discuss your vocational or collegiate goals, desires or fears with this person. He or she can be very helpful to you.

Sometimes parents seem to have their children's future all planned out. They may try to persuade you to take a certain job or choose a certain college out of their own desires for you. Usually, however, your parents want you to do what's best for you. Ask them for help or advice. Discussion of such an important issue may help them get to know you better as a person also. Try to share your goals, hopes and fears with them. Don't forget—they once were faced with the same predicament themselves.

Just a few words on competition (more later). Too often teenagers are so caught up in the prestige of a college or the amount of money that a job or trade school will bring them that they forget what is most important. You and your friends will face the future at around the same time. Try to talk about it with them as well. You will all probably be going through the same thing. Try your best to be there for one another and avoid trying to outdo one another.

Finally, try to never lose sight of just whose future it really is. It is hard enough to study and do well in school, but at the same time people want you to begin thinking about what you are going to do with your life. If you're not ready to begin what may be a very long, involved process of finding a college, trade school or full-time work, ask them all to give you space. Concentrating on the present is important too. If you are concerned at this point about the future, use counselors, friends, older brothers or sisters and parents to your advantage. The more people you can talk with, the better the perspective you may get. Above all, take your time; try to relax and let your future be the end product of decisions made thoughtfully and carefully. Who you are and who you become is in your very own hands.

# Stresspoint #6:

## ANGER

*All of the hurt and tears come tumbling out. When will they stop? Fireballs of anger tumble from my mouth. Did I really mean what I said? I try to absorb the tears in my hands. Have I been really this upset? I feel so lost and confused. Why is anger always lonely?*

[*Nancy*]

Some people express anger easily; others keep a lot of anger inside themselves. I think how you express your anger depends on how anger is expressed in your family. Some families seldom express anger directly, some express it often. Some families use physical violence and some use the "silent treatment." Some families have shouting matches and some families have meetings to resolve conflicts. We all learn about anger and its appropriate expression as children in families.

When I was young my own family didn't express anger very directly. We, like many other Christians, somehow had the idea that to be angry was not "nice," not virtuous, not kind, not polite. As I grew older I learned that not expressing anger causes difficulties emotionally. I also learned that Jesus expressed anger when the temple entryway was made into a sort of flea market. In fact he got so mad he turned over the tables and yelled and screamed. So now I figure that if it was O.K. for God's Son to express anger on occasion, it must be O.K. for me too.

Psychology has taught us much. As we said earlier, when anger is stuffed down, unexpressed within us, it easily turns into

22

depression. It also has the potential to build up within us only to explode at a later time (the proverbial "last straw"). And so we can safely say that it is unhealthy emotionally (and even physically sometimes) to repress anger all the time. It needs expression just as any other emotion. It is not a bad emotion, an un-Christian emotion. It simply is one feeling in the broad spectrum of human feelings.

But today we have gone to other extremes from when I was a kid. Now everybody expresses anger more freely with not the same sensitivity for the feelings of others that we seem to have had in my family. Feeling the need to "express oneself" is only one need that people have. We also have the need to give sometimes and to live together in harmony. What I'm getting at is that there are times to express anger and times to withhold anger. We can't always be voicing every irritation just as we can't always be repressing the same. For example, if something a family member does irritates you constantly you should really express that feeling. In fact you *owe* the person that because otherwise your anger will manifest itself in small ways and the person will have no explanation for your behavior (like becoming moody or irritable). But suppose it's something that isn't going to go away . . . suppose it's a habit like a parent smoking or the sloppiness of a brother or sister. Suppose that you ventilate your anger but the situation doesn't change. You can't keep expressing hostility. This is why I say that there are certain frustrating situations which we have to accept in life.

So when to express your anger? Ideally when you feel it, not two weeks later. To whom? To the person who makes you angry, not to a third party. That just is not as satisfying. How often? I don't know; just use your judgment. When something *really* upsets you you should express your anger, as when you feel that if you don't say something then your feelings will eventually build up to an explosion. So you have to know yourself too. If you express your anger *when felt to the person* there isn't the need to always yell. Just to state your angry feelings will be satisfying enough.

To deal with anger within yourself I suggest that you follow these basic rules to emotional health:

1. admit to yourself that you *are* angry (when angered);
2. express your anger in a rational way at the time you feel the anger;
3. express the anger to the person at whom your anger is directed; if this is impossible, express it to a third party or alleviate the emotion by physical activity like running or hitting a punching bag;
4. "let go" of the anger after it is expressed; don't nurse grudges or hurt feelings;
5. negotiate solutions to mutual problems, allowing for give and take.

Many conflicts can be resolved if people will be mature and each party gives a little to arrive at a compromise. Try this if you haven't before. Lastly, if you find yourself angry all the time, ready to lash out at anyone, or if you find yourself depressed for long periods of time, talk with a guidance counselor or a counselor in the community. Anger and depression to some degree are normal. But severe, extended feelings of either might need a little outside help.

# *Stresspoint #7:*

## FRIENDS AND RELATIONSHIPS

> *When you part from your friend,*
> *you grieve not;*
> *  For that which you love most in*
> *him may be clearer in his*
> *absence, as the mountain to the*
> *climber is clearer from the plain.*
>
> [*Kahlil Gibran,*
> *"The Prophet"*]

Throughout our lives we will no doubt have many friends. If we really think about who our friends are, we realize that each one is so different from another. Each friend fulfills in us a different kind of need. Who are our real friends, though? How can a person be sure that a friend is truly a friend? The word friend tends to be taken for granted a bit, perhaps used too lightly. We all have our own definition of friendship. For a moment try to think about what your personal definition might be. What are the adjectives you would use to identify the ingredients of friendship?

Relationships with friends can be many things to a teenager: a person to share with, talk, laugh or cry with, a good time buddy or a spiritual level of friendship. Let's begin our discussion by talking about an important ingredient of friendship—trust. Whom can we really trust? You may be wondering if you can trust a certain friend with something important to you. For every concern you may have, let's remember that your friend probably has the same concern. Before thinking about whether you can trust a

25

friend, think about whether you yourself can be trusted. To have a friend, you must be a friend first. Sure, it's easy to trust people with little issues, but when is it safe to trust someone with something dear to your heart? You may have been "burned" in the past by a friend you really trusted. Although such an experience brings pain and feelings of betrayal, we must see that there is growth from that.

A short while ago I was counseling a young woman who was the child of an alcoholic father. For years she carried this burden alone, in silence. Living in a family where a member has this kind of illness is very difficult. She talked to me often about it but was never able to talk to her friends about it. I encouraged her not to feel ashamed and to share her world with someone she trusted. After a while she was able to discuss why so often she was angry and depressed with one of her closest friends. She said that her friend listened and felt badly for her. A few months later she found out that her friend had told someone else. She came to me that week shattered by her friend's betrayal. She said she knew she shouldn't have told anyone but me. She was angry at me for suggesting that she share this part of her life with another person. I understood her anger and asked her if she told her friend how all of this made her feel. She said she couldn't even look at her friend yet. I encouraged her to share with her friend how hurt she was. Unfortunately, she never did.

This young person will no doubt find it very difficult to trust again. The pain she felt over her private life being revealed to another was very real. I pray she will learn to trust again at some point in her life. I shared this story with you to show the effect we have on one another. Many of us want friends, but to want a friend we have to be a friend. If you have ever had the joy of a friend trusting himself or herself with you, you must realize the responsibility that accompanies such a close bond.

Honesty is another element of friendship you may think about. Feeling close to someone does not always come easily. It usually requires mutual openness and honesty. Think now about how open and honest you are with yourself and your friends. How often do you share your feelings with your friends? Are your friends honest and open with you? If you can say yes to these questions, then fantastic. If you can't, you may need to think some more about the type of relationships you really have. Too often friends get caught up in pettiness. By pettiness I mean two friends allowing smaller unimportant things to come between them. Usually these small things, if not talked about openly, can lead to bigger problems. I know it's tougher to do than say, but keeping the lines of communication open for the honest exchange of thoughts and feelings can help avoid many problems and mis-understandings.

The ingredients which help formulate important relation-ships with people in our lives are also important when we think about our relationship with God. First you can decide if a friend-ship with God is something you want. God is there for you, wait-ing for you to trust, care and honestly invest in him. When we think of our other friendships we think of a "two way street" sit-uation. God, however, is one who doesn't care about what you give back. God is there for you at all times, under any circum-stance. Prayer is one way of cultivating a relationship with God. God will never give you a reason to be shy or distrustful. He is waiting with open arms for your friendship. Yes, we often turn to God when the stresses of friendship become too great to bear, but how often do we simply turn to him as a friend, to trust, love and share our lives? Friendships find many forms in life, but being a real, true, dedicated friend to someone is perhaps one of the great-est gifts a person can give to another. And despite any of the pain that growth in friendship causes, it is always worth it in the end if it means that we truly have a companion for life's journey.

# *Stresspoint #8:*

## PROBLEMS AT HOME AND IN SCHOOL

*I am walking down that street again.*
*My street.*
*I am the only one.*
*No one else has ever*
*No one else will ever*
*Walk that lonely street.*

[*Mark*]

If you had to pinpoint some of your most recent problems, where would they be? Chances are a few, if not more, could be found in school or at home. Each kind of problem carries with it its own form of stress. I won't attempt to address every possible type of problem a teenager could come up against, but I will try to identify a few and offer some suggestions to help reduce the likelihood of increased stress. At this moment you are probably carrying around a few problems of your own. If you think about it, the problems you have probably all differ in degree. Let's first distinguish a problem from an aggravation.

Aggravations occur in one's life almost every day. Whether you stub your toe, don't care for a way of dress, or find the smell of your chemistry lab offensive, aggravations are ever present. It is these types of things you encounter daily that you should try to ignore or at least not let get you too up-tight and stressed. A problem, on the other hand, could range from a broken leg to a death in your family. Whatever problem is the issue, it is much health-

28

ier to address and deal with it than to simply ignore the fact that it exists. If you are the kind of person who lets the smaller things in life really get you down, then you probably will begin to feel more stress.

One very healthy way to prevent small problems from becoming larger is to talk about them with someone. Many teenagers live such a fast-paced life that they often never take the time to slow down and think about their problems. Before you know it a few different problems begin to add up, and then dealing with them can become harder and more painful. Keeping a problem to yourself is not easy. What you may forget is that there is someone in your life willing to listen to you who you may be denying the chance to help you. There aren't too many people capable of reading minds, so often the only way you will be able to find someone to listen and help is by your own reaching out. I think there is too much emphasis on being or appearing to be "strong." Don't think you are "weak" if there comes a time in your life when you need to talk about something that may be troubling you. The ability to reach out when you are hurting is a beautiful one. Certainly someone in your life has come to you with a problem and you were glad to listen.

A common thread of problems for teenagers involves things that happen at school. You may have difficulty with a certain subject or class. If so, why pretend it doesn't exist or that it will magically go away? Any worthy teacher should be open to your getting extra help in a given subject. Again the responsibility of dealing with this type of problem rests with you. You must have the maturity to realize that your grades are not making it and then seek help. If there is a personal problem contributing to your doing poorly, your teacher will not know unless you let him or her know. If the problem lies within your relationship with the teacher himself or herself, do your best to talk with that teacher about how he or she makes you feel. If you can't do that, talk it over with a guidance counselor or a teacher you trust. The main thing is to do something. Education is a gift you should take seriously, since it will play a large part in the rest of your life.

We all know that there are going to be times when problems will occur at home. Parents and other family members can make life confusing for teenagers, perceiving them as "too young" for certain things, yet putting very adult-like responsibilities and expectations on them. Because each family is unique, so too are the circumstances surrounding family problems. We talked earlier about the importance of communication in all relationships. Problems in communication tend to be at the root of many domestic quarrels. By letting family members know how you feel about your problems, you are giving them and yourself a chance to work things out. Letting things fester inside of you does no one any good. Respectfully discussing how a family problem makes you feel is a sign of adult-like behavior and shows concern and love instead of the disinterest and lack of caring often perceived when you are silent. Of course not all family matters can be discussed successfully, and after trying you may feel the need to get outside help. Again, it is always best to talk to someone who may be able to lend support to you.

Remember, no issue is ever one-sided. I'm sure there are times when you may naturally blame another or yourself for your problems. As mentioned earlier, when problems arise, try to slow yourself down and think. Feel within yourself how best to handle it, remembering the people involved. Certainly there are some things we can deal with on our own, and if you feel capable, do so. There may be times when it seems that no one cares or can help, but before you decide this, think of the people who love you. Unfortunately we often forget that God always cares for us. How often do you bring your problems to God? He is there for you, although many only turn to him when desperate, as a last resort. Jesus Christ will always be able to carry your burdens. Try praying for strength when life seems too hard and problems bring you stress.

# CONSUMERISM

*Simplify in order to live intensely in the present moment. . . . You need so little to live, so little to welcome others. When you open your home, too many possessions are a hindrance rather than a help to communion with others.*

[*Brother Roger of Taizé*]

*I*n the last five years we in North America have become increasingly materialistic. One way this is evident is the concern of many young people to succeed financially. Now this is not just a question of wanting to be secure—to have enough to eat and drink, to have a decent home and enough money for a happy family life. These aspirations have been the hope of every generation. No, it seems that many young adults today don't just want a moderate amount of material prosperity and a middle class lifestyle. They want to become *very* rich, have *many* material things and live a very materialistic lifestyle. It's interesting that we have made the word "success" today synonomous with making good money. When we say someone is very "successful," we mean that he or she is financially well off.

So you ask, and it's a fair question: Is there anything wrong with being rich? Is there anything un-Christian about it? Our answer would have to be first of all "yes"—but secondly "no." Let me explain. There have been holy people who were rich, like St. Thomas More and St. Elizabeth of Hungary. It's not how much money we have; it's our attitude toward it that makes us Christian

31

or un-Christian. If we become obsessed by it or very selfish with it, then that obviously is not good. On the other hand, if money not only makes our own lives more gracious but also helps us to reach out in generosity to others, then we can be rich and Christian at the same time. But this is not easy. Money has the capacity to catch us in its grip. Jesus was referring to that when he said that it is impossible to serve both God and money and that it is very difficult (he didn't say impossible) for a rich person to enter heaven. It's difficult because money has such potential to consume our energies and desires.

But let's look at money in a different way. I don't see the desire of so many kids to "make it" financially as evil in itself. It's wonderful in some senses to live in a society which both allows and encourages personal ambition. My problem with the money-orientation of so many young people is that other values get second place . . . values that are more important than money. I mean such basic values as having good friendships and relationships; being a good family member; being a caring person about the suffering of so many in our society; being a compassionate follower of Jesus Christ. I see the preoccupation with financial success taking all the energies of many good young people and making them forget or put in second place the values that are deeper and more lasting. And this is very sad to behold. It is spawning a generation that seems to live on a more surface level and which relegates people to a subordinate role to success.

This consumerism causes much stress for many. College students who are very inclined to the helping professions like nursing, teaching and social work get deflected from that path by the desire for more money. Young people inclined toward a people-oriented career and who have so much to offer others go into a business or scientific career solely for the purpose of becoming rich. The idea that money will make a person happy is so wrong; look at all the rich people who have lived miserable lives. No, happiness comes from fulfilling who you are meant to be in life and from meaningful human interaction. But the pressure is on from so many quarters in our society to "make it" and to be a "success."

All I can say is to resist. Resist parents and peers and anyone else who pressures you into a "financially rewarding" career for its own sake. I'm not saying to be poor because that certainly doesn't bring happiness. I'm saying: Look to your deepest self to discover what you *really* want in life and go for it despite what any other voices around you may clamor.

## DATING AND SEX

*Being a man or woman involves us in much more than reproduction. . . . Our gender gives us a fundamental orientation toward all reality. Our self-images, as well as the roles, expectations, and limits society places on us, are largely rooted in the fact that we are male or female. . . .*

> [*Richard Reichert,*
> *"Sexuality and Dating"*]

When considering some of the most prevalent concerns of teenagers, I think we can all agree that dating is among them. On any given day, in any high school, discussions about who is dating whom or who dumped whom can be heard. What many people don't understand is that dating can not only be fun and exciting, but very stressful as well. One of the most important moments in a teenager's life is when he or she finally experiences the "first date." If you haven't had your first date yet, be patient; the day will come. If you have, this section will attempt to give all of those interested in dating a few things to ponder.

There's a lot of pressure put on adolescents today to begin dating. Some teenagers may panic if by the age of sixteen they haven't had a date yet. Relax; it's only a matter of time before someone will ask or accept. Of course your parents may have strong ideas about when you should start dating. Do your best to understand that this is a natural way for a parent to feel. You may perceive this as none of their business or feel that they're just being nosy. Try to understand that they love and worry about you. The rules or questions you may not like stem from concern for you.

Many times teenagers bring on their own stress when dating. Some feel that they have to have someone popular, smart, athletic or good looking. Don't get caught up in looking for someone your peers think is suitable; date the person who is right for you. Often teenagers will rely on what is known as the other person's "reputation." Usually these reputations are fabricated and do not justly represent what kind of person someone really is. Trust your own judgment and feelings before you trust what someone else might say.

We all have our own special values and beliefs. Try to rely on yours when dating. It is normal to worry about what your date might say if you don't believe in what your date does. Don't sell your special friend short; if your boyfriend or girlfriend has respect for you, he or she will allow you your own viewpoints. One of the major stresses on young people today is the area of sex. Whether you are male or female, you may find yourself out on a date with someone who is a little "faster" than you. Remember, God created you as a very special individual. Believe in your own heart and don't do something you are not sure about and may regret one day. Don't allow pressure to cause you to give yourself away to a person quickly and cheaply.

The Catholic Church feels strongly that young people should not have sex before marriage. This statement is not made to make life difficult for people or to be strict. No, the wisdom of the Church's dealing with human problems down through the ages makes it feel that young people open themselves up to deep pain and heavy commitments when they engage in sexual activity. So it's to help prevent teenagers from getting hurt themselves or hurting others that the Church takes a strong stand on the issue. The Church's viewpoint is the ideal for which we should strive. But when we fail, we don't need to feel tons of guilt. We just need to try harder in the future to be the best person we can possibly be.

If pressure for sex is an issue between you and the person you are dating, try to talk to someone about it. You may not yet feel comfortable talking to the person you are involved with, but you may need to discuss it with someone. A brother, sister, a parent or friend may be able to offer some reassurance on the matter. If you are not comfortable talking about sex with the person you are dating, chances are you don't know that person well enough. We all have the need for intimacy and warmth, but these needs should be addressed slowly and sensitively and can be met in ordinary friendships.

When a relationship reaches the point where sex becomes involved, people increase their chance of being hurt and deceived. How can we be solidly sure that a person loves and cares about us? If you are going to equate sex with caring you may find that you've made a mistake. It is far better to develop a more trusting, lasting and secure relationship before you make this kind of step. Sex is a huge commitment, linked to a permanent commitment to the other person. Reflect within yourself if at your age you are ready and mature enough to live up to such an intense commitment as marriage.

Pregnancy is also a real possibility when teenagers involve themselves in sexual relationships. One mistake or hasty decision could cause you, your mate and both families tremendous stress. Unless you are ready to be a parent and a husband or wife, you must consider this a negative consequence for your actions. Pregnancy too often forces young people to change their lives so completely that they regret ever having had sex. Neither is it fair to bring a child into the world where there isn't the stability of a family life in which he or she can grow up. Don't kid yourself into thinking it will never happen to you because it certainly could.

It is natural for young people to want to explore relationships with those of the opposite sex. We're not suggesting that you shy away from dating or close friendships. Dating will develop naturally with your own maturation. Be yourself always and don't add stress to your life by trying to please other peers. God has given you the gift of life—a gift to be treasured. We can only enjoy relationships if we are honest with ourselves and with others. Rely primarily on your own beliefs and values and listen to the wisdom of adults and of your Church who care so much about your happiness and well-being.

## DRUGS AND ALCOHOL

> *Do you not know that your body is a temple of the Holy
> Spirit, who is in you, whom you have received from
> God? You are not your own; you were bought at a price.
> Therefore honor God with your body.*
> *[1 Corinthians 6:19–20]*

Today as young people progress through their teenage years
there are a few things that each is certain to encounter. One
is alcohol and drugs. I do not wish to imply that every teenager
will try or become involved with alcohol or drugs. Somewhere
along the line, however, most of you reading this have already
been, or will be, in a situation where you will have to decide what
to do when someone offers a drink or drug to you. Try to reflect
for a moment. How well have you handled or will you handle
such a decision?

For each of you a decision to try or avoid trying an illegal
substance is a very significant one. We all encounter the decision
at different times in our lives, ranging from pre-high school years
to adulthood. There is a range of stress involved with this decision.
For some the choice is a simple one. "All of my friends do, so it's
natural for me to." In your group of friends alcohol and drugs
might not be cool, so the choice again is an easy one. For most,
abstaining from or experimenting with drugs involves an individual move with or against what others are doing.

At this point I want to do away with the myth that alcohol

and drugs are two separate items. One definition of a drug is "a substance other than a food intended to affect the structure or function of the body." *Alcohol is a drug.* Let's not kid ourselves and try to justify use of alcohol by saying, "At least I don't do drugs." From here on in, when we use the word drugs, we are also referring to alcohol.

Let's talk a bit about two concerns most people your age have—respect and acceptance. There is stress which often comes along in achieving these. Some people are fortunate to already be accepted and respected by their peers. Sometimes this comes more easily to people blessed with a certain skill, physical quality or outstanding ability. It seems as though everyone accepts someone who possesses one of these qualities. I'm sure you know a person or two like that. The stress to be accepted by friends or new people you meet often breaks down a person to the point that he or she will do something others do without being sure it's what he or she really wants to do. It's a lot easier to meet people or be viewed as a "cool" person at a party when you say yes to what everyone else is doing.

A few years back I was employed by a counseling agency. I worked with many teenagers during this period. One of my clients, named Mark, was having a difficult time in high school and needed to talk to someone about it. He appeared to be a very normal teenager, yet he knew he was depressed more than he wanted to be. He was involved in school sports and had many friends. He explained to me that lately he just wasn't as happy about his life as he used to be. He was having a lot of arguments with his friends and his grades were slipping. He was honest with me about the fact that he drank beer and smoked a little pot on weekends with his friends. He talked about being bored with his routine of going to school all week and just partying on the weekends. He couldn't remember how he began drinking and smoking and didn't see himself as a person with "a problem." He used to say to me, "I don't want you to think I'm a druggie or anything. I just do it because there's nothing else to do, and sometimes it's kind of fun."

Mark was into a routine that many teenagers are in. He had never considered not "partying" in this way. One week he came in and talked about being tired of the same old thing, stating that he wanted to do something different on the weekends. He was afraid that there would be no one with whom to do anything. He explained that he felt most of the people he hung out with really didn't know him for the person he was. When I asked him what he could do to change any of these situations he talked about, he said that he could just stop going out with his group of "party" friends, but again he was concerned that he'd have nothing else to do. Another option he came up with was to continue being with his friends but just stop "partying" with them. He was afraid they would look down on him or feel he thought he was better than they. He wasn't sure he had the strength to do this. He said he would try not drinking or smoking when they went out this weekend.

He came in the following week to tell me that he tried to abstain on Friday night, but his friends thought he was joking when he refused a joint being passed around. "I was trying," he said, "and I made it through most of the night, but I did end up smoking a few hits. I felt like a jerk for not smoking and then I felt like a jerk after I got high." He was confused, but at least he had considered it. He told me of a kid at the party who didn't have a beer in his hand or get high all night. "Everyone was talking to him," he said. The following week Mark didn't do any drugs. He said he went out with his friends and still had a pretty good time. People asked him what was wrong with him, and he said he replied, "I'm not into it." He was shocked that no one really gave him a hard time. As time went on he felt more comfortable being in situations where drugs were around, but not getting involved with them. He was convinced that more people talked to him at parties than they ever did while he was doing what everyone else was doing. He also began to do better in school. He said he was more confident in himself and he felt more mature.

I share this with you to show how young people can stand on what they want to do, on their own value system. All of Mark's fears about how others would perceive him were worse than how others actually saw him. I'm sure Mark felt better about himself when he learned that others would accept him for what he chose to do, and this drastically reduced the stress that had become so much a part of his daily life.

# DIVORCE

> *The family is in flux just when the young person is trying to discover what is constant in his or her self-definition. . . . When the people who have been the primary models for them suddenly change their behavior and their allegiances, the basic ground on which teenagers form their identity is shaken as if by an earthquake.*
>
> [*David Elkind,*
> *"All Grown Up and No Place To Go"*]

It is estimated that America's future will see one out of every two marriages ending in divorce. This appears a very shocking and frightening reality. More and more of us will come to experience divorce in our own families, with relatives or through our friends. You may have already experienced or seen the often unfortunate consequences of divorce. Because this is becoming more and more a part of American culture, we need to be able to cope with the stress accompanying the separation of the family. This section will attempt to provide you with some ways to handle this stress within your own family as well as ways to help others you care about through this crisis.

Divorce or separation is often a difficult concept to understand. Why, after a number of years of marriage, do a husband and wife decide they don't want each other? You may be wondering how after taking marriage vows of devotion and love two people can just give up. There are hundreds of reasons why people get divorced. In every instance the situation is unique, but it is often confusing to younger people. Keeping a family together is not always such an easy task for a mother and father. For the children involved this can be a very traumatic time. Before continuing our discussion I'd like to make mention of the trauma that separation can bring to a parent's life. Parents often suffer tremendously when divorce or separation occurs. After sharing one's life with another for a number of years the fear of living alone or starting over is a very real one. Teenagers can often be supportive in some way to parents in need. If you feel you are capable of supporting your parents in some way, you may be surprised by just how needy they are for that support.

One common reaction among teenagers is denial. Many teenagers cannot accept that problems between mom and dad are incapable of being "ironed out" in some way. There are many married couples who make it through difficult and unhappy times; however when a relationship ends there are usually a compilation of problems and issues so deep that they are unsolvable, or seem to be. Also we hear of married couples who are unhappy but they are staying together "for the sake of the children." This tends to be more common among parents of young children. Parents of teenagers may feel that their children are old enough now to handle the reality. Whether older or younger, this is a time of sadness and stress for anyone.

Whatever the problems surrounding a break-up are, try to remember that these problems are between your parents. Many teenagers and children of all ages tend to blame themselves for the divorce or separation. This is a very natural thing to do. If you feel this way, talk to someone about it. If you feel that you can't talk to one of your parents, try to seek someone else. Extremely few divorces occur due to the children. To take upon yourself the blame for the family's break-up can be very stressful. Unfortunately you may have to suffer the effects of a divorce, but any honest parent will tell you that you aren't the reason.

It is common for parents experiencing this trying time to turn to their children for support. Ventilation of frustration, anger or hurt is extremely important for them. Unfortunately when parents find a release in their kids it can be very stressful and confusing for a teenager. It is difficult enough for a child to look at the situation objectively. It is natural for a parent who is facing separation from a spouse and perhaps children to talk about the other one. When a teenager hears "bad" things about mom from dad and then vice versa, it is awfully confusing. As a teenager, you need to take charge of your own situation. If you are the victim of this type of manipulation, let your parents know that you don't want to hear about these issues. As mentioned earlier their problems are their own and should not be a burden for you. If their "dirty laundry" is being thrown on your shoulders, it could cause more problems and stress than you deserve. Professional counseling can be a positive alternative for a parent. Taking sides may be what your parent instinctively wants from the children, but it is often a very unhealthy phenomenon of divorce.

Although you personally may not be involved in a separating family, you may have friends or relatives who are experiencing this. It's not easy to know what to do if a friend turns to you and says, "My parents are going to get divorced." What can you as a friend do to help another get through this stress? Perhaps the greatest gift comes through listening. Your friend may be depressed, angry or confused about what is going on at home. You can be a real help just by letting him or her know that you care. If he or she isn't the type of person who talks about problems, perhaps you can be a comfort by indicating that you will pray for him or her.

As I said earlier, each family's situation is different. But no one survives a divorce without a few scars. No matter what circumstances you face, the one thing that can make this crisis easier is communication. When a problem of this magnitude arrives it is important for family members to talk with each other about what they feel. If you or a friend finds that talking about the problem with family is impossible, you may want to think about counseling. No divorce or separation is ever simple or "black and white." Remember that the only one who can pull you through a time like this is you. If you're hurting badly, turn to someone who can help. Express whatever you feel; that in itself may lift pressure as well. Prayers can help. Talk to God about your feelings and hopes, knowing that God always listens.

There is an old saying that time heals all wounds. A rift in a family may never heal one hundred percent . . . in fact it probably won't. But things can get better. During the intense stress caused by the separation of your parents, try to keep a little perspective on the situation. They are both still alive, and where there are human relationships there is always the possibility of improvement. Even though you may feel bitterly angry with or distanced from one or both of your parents at this time, it doesn't mean that with the passing of time you can't work things out. People usually grow from painful situations, and this includes parents.

## COMPETITION

*The woods would be very silent if no birds sang there except those that sang best.*

[*John Audubon*]

Ours is a society that competes. We are economically capitalist, which means that our system thrives on competition. Just as democracy is inbred in North Americans, so too is the spirit of competition. It affects and perhaps "infects" us all. School is probably a place where you experience competition most keenly.

Teachers, parents and administrators usually see as part of their role challenging young people to excel academically. Accepting this challenge is the role of the student who wishes to learn and become successful in our society. To be challenged either by oneself or by others is healthy . . . to be pressured is not. Pressure means that unrealistic demands are made for achievement and for undeserving reasons. For example sometimes parents give in to the temptation to "live through" their children. This means that they want their children to become what they were unable to become: an athlete, a scholar, a financial success, a prestigious person in society. Sometimes parents mistakenly feel that what their teenage children choose to do or not do is a reflection on them. If these pressures exist in your family you need to learn to resist them and be your own person. You may slowly need to educate your parents in this regard. But more often than not the encouragement of adults provides a healthy encouragement to use your God-given potential. The competition comes later when you compare yourself to other kids (athletically, academically, in terms of talents, etc.). In other words the pressure is more typically within us than outside of us. And it comes from a comparison of ourselves with others. It comes from a failure to accept ourselves one hundred percent with a sense of gratitude for all that is uniquely us. This is not to say that *all* competition is unhealthy. Competition can be fun and adventuresome on a team, in class, in society. When does it become unhealthy? Well, probably when we take the "contest" itself too seriously as an end in itself. Competition is helpful when it spurs us on to do better, but not when it makes us obsessive about "winning" and bitter when we fail. Another signal that competition has become unhealthy is when we feel a pressure that eats away at us . . . a pressure that produces anxiety and unrest, a pressure that consumes us. This distortion of competition we need to resist.

Cooperation is a much more healthy focus to have in life than competition. It's also much more Christian. Do you ever remember a time in the Gospels when Jesus wanted to achieve more than others or win something at the expense of others? I don't think you could find one. But you can find plenty of examples where Jesus taught cooperation. Do you remember the place in Matthew's Gospel where Jesus tells us that if people want to borrow your shirt, you should give them your coat as well, and when they want you to walk one mile, you should walk two miles with them? Jesus had much more to say about giving in to others and forgetting our own selfish concerns than he does about winning and getting the edge on other people. While there isn't anything wrong in itself with some degree of competition in relationships and in society, competition is not a very high virtue in the Christian life. We in North America have made the competitive spirit into a value of much higher rank than it deserves in Christian nations. And thus we have to be very careful in our individual lives not to let a competitive attitude creep into our daily actions and govern them.

The point of this book is the search for peace of heart. Peace of heart comes from freedom. Freedom is a feeling within us, and it comes to us when we seek the truth, live honestly and lovingly, and let go of things that drag us down like excess baggage. One thing that drags many young people down is the pressure to compete. To let go of this pressure isn't something you can do once and for all. It's a process. Growing in freedom is a process that takes a lifetime, but it has to begin somewhere. It begins by trying to maintain a sense of perspective which means keeping things in their proper place . . . not letting unimportant things grow in importance. A good way for a follower of Jesus to keep perspective is to read a little bit of the Gospel every day (we'll talk about this later in the book). Talking about the pressures we feel is another way to keep things from building up within us. We need the viewpoints of other trusted people to keep our own viewpoints in line.

# *Stresspoint #14:*

---

## MORE ABOUT STRESS IN SCHOOL

> *You don't always know who you are, and when you feel depressed or angry, trigonometry is the furthest thing from your mind. Also you probably don't care what the atomic number of nitrogen is when you are experiencing trouble with your girlfriend or your application for admission to your dad's old college has been turned down.*
>
> *[John]*

Your history teacher assigns the class a ten page term paper, your English teacher wants five books read by the end of the quarter, your math teacher assigns problems every night and homework, and your science project is due in two weeks. What feeling is triggered in you after reading this? Most likely either pressure or panic. Of all the stresses a teenager faces, that of academics can be the scariest. Have you ever felt as though a gray cloud follows you through each year of high school? Can't wait till that glorious day of graduation comes and you can fondly wave goodbye to your high school halls?

The institution of school offers much to teenagers. There are peer and adult relationships, authority figures, theater, sports, hobbies, a chance for a bright future, and, of course, education and growth. Let's talk first about the academic pressure all teenagers face. No matter how efficiently you handle your assignments, it seems as though another awaits you just around the corner. There is absolutely nothing you can do to change this.

You can, however, develop a schedule whereby you take on a little at a time, thus not allowing too many things to build up. One recommendation you might try is to "nip" away each day at your load of assignments. The key to this strategy is beginning assignments due further down the road as quickly as possible. Too often students have a paper assigned in three weeks and don't begin until a few days before it's due. Cramming for exams or assignments adds a double stress. By waiting until the last minute to begin to prepare, you have that gray cloud I spoke of earlier hanging around because you know eventually you must do it. Why bring extra pressure on yourself? By getting a good start you can at least feel you've done something and made progress. Secondly, it is frustrating to try to cram a semester's worth of studying or three weeks of writing and research into a few days or an evening. For this period of time you're most likely to feel greater pressure to finish. When information is absorbed slowly and thoroughly, we tend to learn and remember more than when we are stressed and jam our brains with too much all at once.

We all have our own styles of managing our school lives. Your future is your own, and as you grow older you'll tend to experience fewer and fewer people around to help you develop. Take advantage of the availability of your teachers and school counselors. These people do care about what and how you learn, so trust some of them with your hopes and dreams. Take pride in your future. Whatever you will someday become finds its roots in your personal education. Education is a gift; if you throw it away or take it too lightly, it may come back to haunt you. Developing good habits while in high school can help you in anything and everything you do when older. Colleges as well as most jobs held by adults have their own types of deadlines and pressure to achieve. Learn now to handle these hard realities of school because they prepare you for life . . . they really do.

Distractions can make academic management and achievement difficult. It's too easy to say, "Set your priorities on school," when there are so many other things in your life which are important as well. Juggling stress in friendships, relationships, work and family life isn't always easy. Again time management comes into play. If you have exams or assignments, you must find a way to do what you have to around your work schedule. This may cut into your social schedule. Relationships with friends are very important to a happy life as well. They also may help reduce stress in your life, but you may find that you need to cut down on how much time you spend with friends when compared to the time you have to study. Trying to do too much in a day or a week can run you into the ground if you aren't careful and will most likely affect how well you do in school.

In the end the whole problem of time and stress is a matter of taking control in one's life. "He flunked me" is a statement that reflects a sense of having no control. School doesn't happen *to* you; you make it happen. All the balancing of various responsibilities a young person faces is possible if you're willing to take charge. Accepting responsibility and taking charge requires an emergence from adolescence to adulthood. And so the question of stress in school could be but a symptom of a deeper issue: Are you willing to grow up and take responsibility for your life? Well, it's something to think about.

## CHANGE AND DEATH

*What lies behind us and what lies before us are tiny matters compared to what lies within us.*
[*Ralph Waldo Emerson*]

There was an ancient Greek philosopher who said, "You can't go into the same river twice." Heraclitus meant by this that things are constantly in flux or changing . . . that we can never cling to reality so that it doesn't change. In some ways you probably can't wait for certain changes in life: getting older, being out on your own, having your own car or home . . . it might be you wish that these could be yours immediately. But there are other changes in life which we don't like . . . which cause us a lot of pain and stress.

One example of a difficult change is that of a relationship which should end. I'm thinking of Ronnie and Sue. Ronnie is a good-looking kid and Sue was homecoming queen. Ron was an unmotivated student and after graduation decided to remain in his home town to work as a clerk in a liquor store. Sue, however, a very bright girl anxious to get into her career, went to New York City to college. Their lives, a year after high school, are going in two different directions. And yet on weekends they try to keep their relationship as it was in school. They are trying to hold onto the way things were because both of them care for each other and because they are afraid of changing. A change in human relationships is often tough to undergo.

Another example of a stressful change is an unwillingness to "grow up." Some kids prefer the youthful existence where there are no responsibilities, no commitments, no goals. As these young people become juniors and seniors in high school they may pay little attention to academic pursuits. This unwillingness to mature and change can also manifest itself in terms of not being responsible in relationships . . . or not being responsible at work. Accepting the world of adulthood is definitely a big change.

So how to cope with all these changes? Well it might sound weird at first, but I think that much of it has to do with our attitudes toward death. Death, you see, is the ultimate change which most of us greatly fear, particularly at a young age. St. Paul says that "life is not ended but merely changed." In other words, death is not really an ending. A friend of mine likes to explain death as a being reborn into a new state of life. She speaks of addressing a little embryo within a mother's womb and saying to it: "Hey, come on out of there. Let's go to the beach today. We'll walk along the shore; we'll build sand castles and even go swimming! We'll have a wonderful time." If he could respond, the little babe within the mother's womb would say: "Shore, sand, swim? I have no idea what you're talking about. I'm going to stay right here where it's nice and snug and warm." And we would respond: "Oh, if only you knew how glorious life is out here!"

At birth, of course, the baby is expelled from the mother's womb, and its eyes are open to a glorious, new world.

There is a comparison between the birth of the child and the extension of our lives in heaven. If the saints in heaven could speak so that we could hear them, they might say such things as: "Oh, hurry and join us! We're having a wonderful time where we are." And we, in typical human fashion, would respond: "Oh no, we don't want to go. We don't want to come. We're too secure. We're enjoying our lives here on earth too much." But when we have our second birth, when we are expelled from the womb of this life, our eyes will behold new and glorious sights.

So to summarize, I'm saying that as mature young people

you have to learn to both accept and expect change as a part of life. Death, of course, is the ultimate change. By giving up trying to manipulate life so that things can stay as we like them, we have to be more into a graceful, interior surrender to the unfolding of human events. Easier said than done, true . . . but practicing this attitude in a conscious way can lead to great reduction in stress.

Since we have been talking about death let me just mention a few words about suicide. This is a route that some kids choose to escape a stressful life, but it isn't a good choice. Why? First, because death is so final; there is no undoing of death. Second, it is unfair and cruel to their friends, to the people who love them and care about them. And lastly it indicates an immaturity in handling the stresses and problems of life. People with stress, as we will discuss in the "Stressbreakers" section, need to *talk out* what's going on with a person who can be a good listener, a helpful friend or counselor. It's by keeping so much pain locked inside that we become overloaded by life's stress. So if you feel overwhelmed by problems and/or if suicide crosses your mind (to *think* of suicide is very normal), talk to someone whom you feel may be able to help you. Talk to him or her right away. You should be afraid if suicidal thoughts keep crossing your mind. No matter how hopeless or trapped you feel there is always a way out of every difficult situation. Sometimes events change; sometimes our attitudes about them do. So be mature and go for help. Don't let everybody down who cares for you in this life.

## Part II

## STRESSBREAKERS

# *Stressbreaker #1:*

## SHARING FEELINGS AND HONESTY

> *"Real isn't how you are made," said the Skin Horse. "It's a thing that happens to you. When a child loves you for a long, long time, not just to play with, but REALLY loves you, then you become Real."*
>
> *"Does it hurt?" asked the Rabbit.*
>
> *"Sometimes," said the Skin Horse, for he was always truthful. "When you are Real you don't mind being hurt."*
>
> *"Does it happen all at once, like being wound up," he asked, "or bit by bit?"*
>
> *"It doesn't happen all at once," said the Skin Horse. "You become. It takes a long time. That's why it doesn't often happen to people who break easily, or have sharp edges, or who have to be carefully kept. Generally, by the time you are Real, most of your hair has been loved off, and your eyes drop out and you get loose in the joints and very shabby. But these things don't matter at all, because once you are Real you can't be ugly, except to people who don't understand."*
>
> [Marjorie Williams "The Velveteen Rabbit"]

Perhaps the most important element in a peaceful existence is honesty. Honesty between two people is a beautiful thing to experience. Honesty with ourselves is often difficult. Honesty with God is essential. What exactly do I mean when I speak of honesty? The word encompasses so many different ideas: truth-

57

fulness, sincerity, and genuineness. Why is honesty so important and why is it one important concept when considering a way to break stress? Have you ever had an encounter with someone who isn't being honest with you? It is usually an unpleasant, often sad experience to have. Honesty is the one quality everyone respects in others and one we all recognize immediately if we ourselves possess it.

Real honesty begins within. How can people be genuine and sincere when they haven't become in touch with themselves? We discussed values and morals earlier in this book, and we stressed the importance of carrying out our own beliefs. There will be, or perhaps already have been, times in your life when you've done something you just don't feel right about. Whatever the situation was that caused you to bend your beliefs about what is right in your heart, think about how it made you feel. It may have made you uneasy, but did you take time to experience the feeling or did you simply brush it away and try to justify it? Were you honest with yourself or did you deceive yourself? Often things that hurt us we dismiss too easily. Taking time to think how an argument, break-up or loss made us feel is a way of being honest with ourselves. No one of us is perfect, but we often have trouble accepting our failures or wrong-doings, thus kidding ourselves. Feelings such as guilt, rejection and unhappiness can cause us pain. Be honest with yourself about the way you feel before finding a way to recover.

Honesty with others is an extremely risky endeavor. You may feel that too much honesty with self and especially with others opens you up for disappointment and hurt. What you should try to realize is that revealing yourself sincerely to others is a wonderful gift to yourself and others as well. Just as you know when someone is being honest with you, chances are that your sincerity can be detected. Your genuine self can be the key to a stronger friendship. There are times when "masks" make relationships safer for people. Feel yourself to be a gift to others, not something to be hidden by a false, untrue self. If there is stress between you and a parent or friend, the open expression of feelings may be the refreshing requirement needed to break down the barriers or misunderstandings. Strength is something most people admire in others, but what you may not realize is that showing our weaknesses and feelings in an open way takes tremendous strength. Anyone who knows, loves and cares about you will see through you anyway, so why waste time hiding behind false facades?

Our society doesn't always make it easy to express sincerity and honest emotions. How often have you seen someone who is either "macho," "brainy," "hoodish," or "stuck up"? Are these people *completely* as they appear to be, or are they hiding qualities that may be too risky to reveal to others? It's a lot safer to present yourself in one of these ways instead of as a sensitive, caring, hurting or needy person. Aside from handshakes or affectionate slaps on the back, how often do you ever see two guys even touch each other? How often is it safe for anyone to cry, be weak, feel helpless and down or even too happy? Think about what you can do in your own relationships to help decrease the stress a frightened person might feel over being his or her true self. You are your own person and surely need some defense mechanisms to survive, but striving to do away with facades in your life could help reduce some stresses.

Spiritual development is a struggle which brings growth in self and with God. If you desire to grow spiritually, ask in prayer for strength. God knows what your life is like and knows all about you. It is his wisdom and guidance you can always turn to when a problem or stress becomes overwhelming. Open your heart to God, for he is waiting with acceptance for you. Don't think you need to protect or hide anything about yourself from God. When guilt overcomes you or despair burdens you, share it with God. It does no good to shy away from baring your soul to him, for his love is non-judgmental and unconditional. Freedom of spirit and from all pressure can be felt if you allow him to embrace your concerns. Only if we are honest and trusting of God can he help to comfort. Your spirituality, as well as your relationship with God, is enhanced by honesty. He trusts you enough to let you make mistakes, and he loves you enough to always accept your honesty. By openly sharing your life with God, a fresher sense of self will be found.

Look around you, at the people in your life. Is there a need to hold feelings so bottled up inside you? You are loved by family, friends and God. Whether financial, personal, familial or academically related, all you can count on by not talking out feelings is frustration, loneliness and stress. No matter what has "got you," there is a way to talk it out. Holding our lives inside of us can lead to outbursts of crying, tantrums, violence or psychological problems. Think of the starving or the dying who have no choice but to suffer. You do have a choice; there is always hope and relief in sight. Once you take the risk to share a feeling or issue with another person or God, you are on your way to a reduction of tension.

This entire book's emphasis has been to point out the healthiness of genuine openness, caring, reaching out and love. When we love we are closer to ourselves, others, and God. Christ encouraged people to share feelings and lives together. Prayer offers us reassurance and hope, but these can also be found when we open our hearts to the people in our lives. Talking out feelings is so helpful, and it is also a very holy act. Whether you listen or are in need of a loving ear, chances are that there is one nearby, and there is always one in God.

# Stressbreaker #2:

## DIET AND EXERCISE

*Every athlete in training submits to strict discipline
in order to be crowned with a wreath that will not last;
but we do it for one that will last forever.*

[*1 Corinthians 9:25*]

### Diet

"You are what you eat." How true this is! When we eat balanced and nutritious meals we feel better. Because we feel better we are more able to cope with the hassles and problems of everyday life. But when we overeat we feel lethargic, tired and sometimes depressed. Many of us give in to the "fast food" syndrome. Eating food isn't just a physical reality; it has a social dimension as well. Meals are meant to be eaten with others because sharing food together is one of the most basic human events we can do together. That's why the evening meal or Sunday dinner is so sacred in the eyes of many parents . . . because they know how eating together can add to family closeness. Eating "on the run" or at fast food chains breaks down this type of social interaction.

When we eat a balance of fats, protein and carbohydrates we will feel better. Feeling better reduces stress in life. We need a good portion of fresh vegetables, fruits and fruit juices for good health. We should try to keep to a minimum our consumption of red meat, junk food and sweets. Consult your health teacher in school for more particular information.

A word here about anorexia (starving oneself) and bulimia (gorging on food and then purging). In our culture today there is a high value on a slim figure. Young women especially want to look beautiful, which our society in North America says means being thin. This obsession with being thin is a creation of the marketing world. Our size has little to do with who we are or how beautiful we are. Anorexia is a very dangerous illness, and it should be attended to immediately. If you find yourself skipping meals, refusing food and being over-concerned about your size, you really need to talk to some adult who can help you. You could be headed toward anorexia. Also if you find yourself eating in binges followed by vomiting you could be headed toward bulimia. This is often kept a dark secret, but the trouble with this is that the disease will progress if it isn't confronted. "Overeaters Anonymous" is helpful in this situation, as is any professional counselor. Anorexia and bulimia require help because both are life-threatening illnesses.

A final comment about eating properly: Not only do you feel better by eating properly, you are also caring for your God-given health. As science reveals to us the close connection between heart disease, cancer and a poor diet, we need to assume a more responsible attitude toward proper eating. To eat poorly is in a sense being self-destructive. We know today that health problems, like a high cholesterol level, start at a young age. We know that a high dosage of junk food can contribute to depression. Take responsibility now for who you are (your body) and how you feel.

### Exercise

Have you ever been under so much pressure that you've just wanted to scream? Of course if people ever get a glimpse of you doing this, they may think you're a bit "wacky," but it usually feels great. There is a lot to be said for releasing our bottled-up stress in a physical way. Too many teenagers unknowingly are so stressed that violence becomes a physical way of release. Fighting is no way to handle stress. As an alternative, exercise is a healthier way to break stress. Some of you may experience this through sports teams. Whether you consider yourself an athlete or not, all people can do something for their bodies.

Exercise serves two very valuable purposes. It not only helps to keep our cardiovascular system and bodies fit, but it subconsciously reduces stress for some individuals. For some, exercising as part of a group fills the need for companionship, while others prefer the peace and quiet of their bedroom or the open road. Stretching tired, tensed muscles is a good way to start your exercises. By stretching slowly and thoroughly you can get in touch with your body and its abilities and limitations. If you stretch consistently each day you'll begin to feel more limber and loose. Sure, you may say that gym class offers enough exercise to your life, but at least be open to its benefits.

Some find that taking a long jog brings them release and silence from a hectic day. Others feel the need to run fast and hard, as in a sprint, to burn off frustration or anger. More and more teenagers are practicing aerobic classes. Music, people, jumping and dancing around really can be a source of release. Aerobic classes are so challenging that it's hard to keep one's mind on the issues of the day. Some of you may enjoy pumping iron as a stress reducer. Put energy and frustration into the weights instead of worrying about what's on your mind. Other aerobic exercises such as swimming increase stamina and health as well. Team sports offer support and friendship as well as healthy ways to improve self-esteem and reduce tension.

I'm not suggesting that you use exercise as a way to prevent yourself from dealing with the concerns in your life. I offer exercise as a way to temporarily take your mind off the things that weigh upon you while doing something good for yourself. Setting goals for yourself and trying to achieve them may help build self-confidence as well. So, get out there and stretch, run, jump, push, pull, climb, swim or ride yourself into a better frame of mind. You may begin to see stress as something you're more "fit" to handle.

## PRAYER

*I believe in water, even when it isn't raining.*
*I believe in the sun, even when it isn't shining.*
*I believe in love, when I feel it not,*
*I believe in God.*

Prayer to God directly is another great way to dispel stress. Probably as a kid you knew of two ways to pray: asking God for things and thanking God for the things. And that's fine for little kids. But as we mature in our understanding of who the Lord is and where he is, we also need to mature in the way that we relate to him which is called prayer. Prayer is simply our communication with God. And just as you no longer see your parents as the dispensers of rewards and punishments but as people to relate to in love and friendship, so too you are hopefully growing out of the "gimme God" syndrome.

Jesus certainly taught us to ask for good things from the Father. He also has assured us of God's attention when we make requests. But that our prayers will be answered to our particular specifications is not guaranteed. That would presuppose a God capable of being manipulated by human wishes. God is our friend, and as such he wants to be with us in our struggles and to give us his Spirit to get us through every difficulty. Our welfare is his concern; he cares for us personally and individually. But to turn him into a sort of spiritual Santa Claus who doles out presents from his magic bag is to really cheapen our relationship with him. Do you do that to any of your other friends—make them constantly give you things? Of course not. We have been created as intelligent creatures with the responsibility to work out our own solutions to life's many challenges. This freedom is the root of our creaturehood. To rob us of it would be to rob us of our humanness. Also, God is concerned that we know he is there for us, that he will be with us in our struggle and that in *his own way* he will answer our prayer for his help. And so this type of maturing in our understanding of asking God for things is extremely important if we are to grow out of our spiritual childhood.

Reflect for a few minutes on this short section from the Gospel of Matthew:

> Ask, and you will receive; seek, and you will find; knock, and the door will be opened to you. For everyone who asks will receive, and he who seeks will find, and the door will be opened to him who knocks. Would any of you who are fathers give your son a stone when he asks for bread? Or would you give him a snake when he asks you for fish? As bad as you are, you know to give good things to your children. How much more, then, your Father in heaven will give good things to those who ask him! Do for others what you want them to do for you: this is the meaning of the law of Moses and the teaching of the prophets (Mt 7:7–12).

The most important part about this passage is: When you ask for something in prayer, do you really believe you will receive it? If you do not believe that Jesus really answers prayers, ask yourself: When you pray for something, do you do it as a sort of last resort, figuring that it probably won't help but at least it couldn't hurt?

What attitude do you have deep-down at the bottom of your heart? Do you have the attitude that Jesus really is going to help you out, or is your deepest expectation that he won't? Many of us, unfortunately, fall into the latter category.

To pray with such a negative attitude can be compared to a person who asks a friend, "Will you help me change this flat tire on my car, even though I don't really believe that you will help me?" How would you feel if someone said that to you? In all probability, you would walk away, saying, "Change the tire yourself, if that's how you feel." Yet, isn't this how many of us treat God when we pray? We are saying, "Help me, Lord, even though deep-down I don't believe you are going to bother with my problem." Who could blame God for not granting such an untrusting request?

A second question to ask is: Are we persistent when we pray? The fact that Matthew uses the three verbs *Ask, Seek, Knock* shows very clearly that prayers are not always answered immediately. Patience and perseverance are often required of us. A close examination of the New Testament miracles tells us that Jesus always demands faith in his ability to cure, and—sometimes—persistence in this faith as well.

Praying is a very direct way to deal with stress. It's taking all my problems, my confusion, my worries, and "dumping them in God's lap." It's turning over my life to God, not as a cop-out (because I still need to use my own inner resources to solve problems) but as a sign of trust. Prayer is saying that I trust that Jesus Christ cares about me enough to be involved in my life. I trust that when I pray to him he will give me strength to cope and the perspective to see choices clearly. Prayer is saying that I am not alone in the universe to face life's challenges, but God is also with me to prop me up with courage and confidence when the going gets tough. Use prayer. It's there for you. Jesus is a best friend who is always there for you. So talk to him.

## MEDITATION

*To be calm and quiet all by yourself is hardly the same as sleeping. In fact, it means being fully awake and following with close attention every move going on inside you. It involves a self-discipline where the urge to get up and go is recognized as a temptation to look elsewhere for what is really close at hand.*

[*Henri Nouwen,*
*"With Open Hands"*]

There's a scene in the movie "Karate Kid II" where we are taught that when life becomes stressful and confusing we should return to the source of life, our breath. There is deep truth to this . . . pausing and taking a few deep breaths can restore a sense of balance. This is a form of simple prayer. By focusing on our breathing we are in touch with the source of life, and for believers this means God. It helps us gain "perspective" to pause like this. To have perspective means to see things as they really are and not in some distorted sense. Think of standing a few inches away from an oil painting as opposed to being several feet away. To see the painting as it truly is requires a little bit of distance. This distancing is what is meant by perspective.

Meditation gives perspective too. It's a way of separating ourselves from all the daily problems and pressures in order to get a grip on ourselves and our direction in life. Perspective is crucial to clear thinking and inner peace. Meditation can be a natural sort of thing unrelated to any particular religion. Many young people have learned meditation not from the Church but from reading about Eastern religions and taking courses in transcendental meditation and relaxation techniques. Breathing deeply is often taught as a good way to begin meditation, and good sitting posture is also helpful so that blood flows properly throughout the body.

*Christian* meditation goes a step beyond natural meditation. It also gives us perspective by giving us Jesus' point of view. St. Paul tells us that we should have the "same mind as Christ Jesus," the same point of view. Christian meditation helps us get there.

Meditation is another kind of prayer. It's a special way of thinking about something. We not only use our minds but we also turn the spotlight of faith on the topic. We can meditate by reviewing a good insight, by recalling all the situations in which God has helped us during our life, or by expanding on an idea that we got when we were in prayer. One of the best ways to meditate is to use a book and to keep the written word in front of us. This method helps us to focus our attention. Perhaps we can keep our thoughts from straying too far. Reading slowly, pausing frequently to talk to God, asking for help—all this can lead to important graces. For meditation you can use just about any book of prayers, poems, or inspirational readings, as long as it really moves you to talk to God.

## Praying the Gospels

The best book for meditation would have to be the Bible. Since that is really a collection of many books, we can make a further choice. That would take us into the New Testament, and among those the preference (especially for beginners) would have to be for the four Gospels. Any one of these Gospels would prove to be excellent meditation material because the words of Jesus are always living. They were spoken for and to us, as well as to the people of those days. Also, unlike other books, the words of the

Gospel can never be exhausted. We can always discover new and deeper meanings in what Jesus said.

### Meditating a Gospel Scene

Let's run through a sample Gospel meditation to see how it can be done. Open your Bible to Mark 4:35–51. Read it over slowly and then let your imagination fill in the details. It is evening, and you are standing in a crowd on the shore of the Sea of Galilee. Jesus is in a boat about to be launched. He wants to go to the other side. Imagine yourself pushing the boat off the sand and then jumping into it along with some of the disciples. The Master is very tired, so he goes to the stern to get some rest. Soon he falls asleep. Meanwhile, the wind has picked up. The waves are getting choppier. Even the experienced fishermen are concerned. The boat is shipping water—yet Jesus sleeps on. If the storm gets worse, you will all go down. You and some of the disciples wake Jesus with the words, "Teacher, does it not matter to you that we are going to drown?" Jesus stands up and tells the wind to be quiet and the waves to be still. And that's what happens. The lake is as smooth as glass, and only the gentlest of breezes touches your cheeks. He turns and looks at you. "Why did you have so little faith?"

What did you feel like when Jesus asked you that? Why don't you trust him more in your life? He will be Savior for each one of us right now—if we only let him.

The Gospel is a wonderful aid toward warding off pressures because it helps us to remember the important values in life. Meditating on the Gospel for five minutes a day can really keep a person peaceful and balanced. The best way to do this is to try to stick to the *same* time of day every day . . . such as first thing in the morning or just before supper or just before bedtime. All the great masters of spirituality suggest that beginners in prayer and meditation really need to set aside a regular time each day so that the *habit* of prayer can develop. Another aid to meditation is journal keeping. A journal is a pad or booklet of empty pages; some people also use a diary. After you meditate for five minutes you simply take another five minutes to record your feelings in your journal. Journal keeping is another way to focus and keep perspective. It also helps us to notice good and bad patterns in our lives if we keep writing over several months.

I want to conclude this section by suggesting some particularly good Gospel chapters to read when you are really feeling "stressed out." When we read the Bible we should just read a few lines at a time, letting the words soak in. It isn't a book we read from cover to cover. So one short section or story from the Gospel is enough for one sitting or day. In fact we may be able to meditate on one section over a few days if it really speaks to our hearts.

The suggestions:
Matthew 5:1–12
Luke 12:33–34
Matthew 6:24–34
Luke 10:38–41
Luke 11:9–13
Mark 4:35–41
Luke 12:2–7
Matthew 11:28–30
Matthew 14:22–32
Luke 15:3–7
John 6:35–37
John 15:1–17

## THE EUCHARIST

*Jesus is in every face.*
*He is every laugh,*
*He is every tear.*

*Jesus is in every heart.*
*He is at every wedding,*
*He is present for every funeral.*

*Jesus is in every soul.*
*He is in the eyes of the naive young children,*
*He is in the hurt, the anguish of an abused child.*

*Jesus is in every mind.*
*He is a new-born baby,*
*He is a dying friend.*

*Jesus is in every squeal of joy,*
*He is in every shriek of terror.*
*He is felt in every embrace,*
*He is present in every war.*

*Jesus is the reason why.*

*Jesus is the who, the what.*

*Jesus is.*

[*Michael*]

The main trouble with the sacraments is that by labeling them we tend to think of them as "things." In reality the word "sacrament" refers to the specialness of the "meeting" between Jesus

Christ and the person. There are many ways we can be united to Jesus, of course: by reading his Gospel, spending time in prayer, helping the poor and needy, and so on. However it has always been believed by the Christian community that there is a special encounter between God and persons at significant moments of the human life cycle. Some of these encounters were spoken about by Jesus himself; some were not. It is now the consensus of our community (the Roman Catholic Church) that there are seven of these special moments.

The word "Eucharist" refers to the most special and intimate union between God and humanity. It is the moment when we literally consume the very person of Jesus Christ under the forms of bread and wine. It's the sacrament that was instituted by Jesus himself at the Last Supper when he told his apostles to eat his body and drink his blood, for by so doing they would live forever.

This sacrament is a very great mystery and beyond our understanding. There's an "old time religion" expression, "Better felt than telt," meaning better experienced than explained if you want to understand it. So it is with the Eucharist (which we usually call "Holy Communion"). By receiving it at Mass we can have a real experience of union with Jesus, and many people who go to Communion regularly can even feel his presence within them in a spiritual sense. The Eucharist is the greatest gift we could have from God, and it gives us much grace.

To "consume" a beloved one is not alien to our psychology. We talk about loving a baby so much we could "eat it up." People who are deeply in love long to be consumed by the other in a spiritual sense or to be able to break the bonds that isolate us from each other as human beings. And so the idea of consuming Jesus should not strike us as strange but rather very much in keeping with human psychology.

The Eucharist is also the source of strength we have to live a loving life because it *is* God who *is* Love. We all know how easy it is to talk about love, and we all know pretty much what it is to act in loving ways. But given our many weaknesses and the frailty of our human condition, we often fail in loving. One of the things the Eucharist does is to help us go on loving when we find it very difficult.

Another understanding of the Eucharist that I want to discuss with you is as a sacrament of healing. This is a meaning that a lot of us forget. We know that the sacrament of reconciliation focuses on the healing of relationships and that anointing of the sick focuses on physical healing. But the Eucharist also is a healing sacrament. I like to think of it as focusing on our own inner healing.

In the Gospels so often we find Jesus healing someone's suffering . . . sometimes physical, sometimes psychological, and sometimes spiritual. Jesus in fact came to heal so that we could, as he said, "have life to the full." But the healing always required faith on the part of the person being healed. This faith requires dependency upon and trust in Jesus.

Jesus is God's presence to human persons; Jesus is the "sacrament" of God. The most special, most intimate way we can experience Jesus is by receiving the Eucharist. When we do this in faith and trust we are turning to Jesus for healing . . . healing from all the stresses we have discussed in this little book. We are giving him our tensions, our anxieties, our confusion and our short-sightedness. We are in a very real way asking Jesus to "touch" us, to give us his peace, his perspective, his patience, his perseverance. We are asking him to help us not feel all fragmented and torn up inside, but rather to feel whole, to feel physically, emotionally and spiritually full of health. This feeling is hard to explain, and so I am reminded again of the old saying: "better felt than telt."

Sad to say, many kids today deprive themselves of the great gift of the Eucharist. Some do so just by their lack of awareness of what Jesus in Holy Communion can do for us and how he can make us feel. These people go to the altar daydreaming or fooling around, talking to their friends or totally distracted. And so as Jesus truly comes into them it hardly means anything at all. It's like having a friend come into your house but you stay in your bedroom ignoring him. Then there are kids who just skip Sunday Mass and so hardly ever receive the Eucharist. They're really depriving themselves of so much without knowing it.

I'm going to make a strong suggestion here. The next time you are really stressed out I want you to get up early and go to Mass, even if it isn't Sunday. And I want you to receive Communion. After Mass I want you to stay in church and let the experience of receiving Jesus really soak in deeply into your being. Talk to him then about all you need in life. I want you to do this not so that you can practice penance or self-discipline, but rather so that you can know the beautiful healing power of God's love—God's personal love just for you.

# FORGETTING ABOUT YOURSELF

*"You have heard that it was said, 'An eye for an eye, and a tooth for a tooth.' But now I tell you: do not take revenge on someone who does you wrong. If anyone slaps you on the right cheek, let him slap your left cheek too. And if someone takes you to court to sue you for your shirt, let him have your coat as well. And if one of the occupation troops forces you to carry his pack one mile, carry it another mile. When someone asks you for something, give it to him; when someone wants to borrow something, lend it to him."*

[*Matthew 5:38–42*]

*B*efore we talk about stress let's talk about what I call the paradox of being a Christian. A paradox is a *seeming* (but not actual) contradiction. The paradox of Christianity is summed up in this one sentence from the Gospel:

Whoever tries to gain his own life will lose it, but whoever loses his life for my sake will gain it.

What Jesus is saying here is that if you are always seeking your own happiness, looking out for "number one," then you will never find what you are looking for. If, on the other hand, you forget about yourself and, for Jesus' sake, try to make *others* happy, then *paradoxically* you will discover happiness yourself. This is a very hard truth for us to hear. Today everybody is so concerned with *self*—self-fulfillment, self-actualization, being "good to yourself." We are known as the "me generation." And yet Jesus says that this self-preoccupation will never achieve happiness. Think yourself of the times you are just wrapped up in your own welfare. Does this bring you real, lasting happiness? Then think of a time you were very involved in relationships and caring for others. Did you find happiness there? Probably you did. This is the type of thing Jesus is talking about. He said that unless a seed (you) falls into the ground and in a sense "dies" it will remain alone. So if you just focus on yourself, you become very lonely. But if you "die" to yourself, forget about yourself like a seed, then eventually you will "bring forth much fruit"—you'll get results. It's very hard to keep this Gospel value alive today. That's where you need the Christian community to keep this truth alive for you. You just can't do it alone in such a selfish civilization.

A source of real worry to a lot of us is having to "die" to our own self in one symbolic sense, not a physical sense. We die to ourselves every time we ignore our own selfish instincts and do something or give up something for another person or group. Every time we give up "our way" of doing something or crush an unkind remark within us or put ourselves out for other people's happiness or comfort, we are dying to ourselves. A beautiful example of dying to oneself is the mother of young children who is so busy nourishing and caring for her little ones that she doesn't even have a moment to think about herself.

For some reason we fear this letting go of our own selfishness. It's as though if we gave in or if we did something for someone else we would lose a part of ourselves by clinging to ourselves, or our viewpoints, our own needs and desires, our own comfort and satisfaction. Paradoxically the message of Jesus, as I have said, is that when we give up our self-interest we discover our true selves. When we give to another we recover something more for ourselves. When we behave unselfishly and in a kindly way toward people we discover who we are. This is a mystery, something beyond our understanding. And yet it is at the heart of Jesus' teaching and life as well as at the core of every major world religion's body of wisdom. Jesus' physical act of dying on the cross so that we might have "life" is the perfect example of the mystery of giving life to others by our little "deaths" to self each day. Rather than fearing this process of self-denial we should learn to practice it often so that it will not frighten us and in order that we may be transformed into our truest selves.

But beyond these reasons, and related to this book, thinking about others reduces our own stress. One reason we get so stressed is because we're so preoccupied with ourselves. Some of us live our lives by constantly looking into a symbolic mirror. By taking the focus away from ourselves we not only fulfill the Christian's purpose but we distract ourselves from ourselves. And *this* kind of distraction is healthy and much needed. We need to realize that other people have problems too and that some of them are much worse than our own. We need to get absorbed in the stresspoints of others in order to gain perspective and insight into our own lives. We have to discover the great feeling of satisfaction and strength that is derived from carrying the burdens of another person. If we all were concerned with relieving one another's stress, what a great world we would have. When you feel the need to "lighten up," get involved in the struggles of somebody else.